Terry Hetherington

# *The Undiminished*

Swansea Poetry Workshop

First Impression – 1997

Published by
Swansea Poetry Workshop
124 Overland Road
Mumbles
Swansea SA3 4EU
Wales

ISBN 0 906480 08 6

The  cover image is reproduced from the author's original.

Typeset and Printed  by John Penry Press, Swansea

*To Aida*

## Acknowledgements

*Arcade, Element 5, The Register, Trails Press* (U.S.A.) *Maximum Load, Picture: Welsh Poets, Radical Wales, The Works* (W.U.W.), *Glas-Nos, The New Welsh Review, Lyric* (**India**), *Come into the Warm, Red Poets' Society, Swagmag.*

# Contents

*Contents continued*

# M.P.

Then were his days,
the reincarnate wolf
pushing through the briar of want.
The thorn pricked his reason,
pained his mind,
and as his thoughts bled fire
fervour fanned the flame,
his tongue boiled.
They came from miles around to hear;
he is our man, they said;
give him the sustenance
of our commitment.
At local elections the cross on the paper
spoke for them.

He answered naked in his progress
to their dream.
Contention haunted him,
he sought out and excised
the feculent eruptions
on the socialist skin of Wales.
The pharisees quailed,
this could not be,
it marred the bland  complexion
of the social whirl.
Send him quickly,
riding high through the fervid valleys
on the eager shout of his people
to a seat in London.

Ten years on he is back to cut a tape,
unveil a plaque:
the suit is immaculate as he takes the rostrum,
he speaks for twenty minutes,
the vocal sound perfect,
each vowel nicely rounded;
the plum has entered his mouth,
evicted the accent.

Pauses practised for effect
cannot be faulted,
he speaks for twenty minutes
but his valley is mute,
the crowding hills brood,
there is nothing to echo.

# Linkage
## (For Troy)

In the peculiar pull of the bloodline,
I have shared a measure
of your three years' existence here,
directing your gaze to the heavens,
and lifting your small frame
to the embrace of foliage.
Rivers you have seen
and the flight of startled birds.
Your body folds down
as you touch some life I do not see.

I know now that all of these are part of you:
you have sloughed the scales from my reasoning,
and I am learning to accept with shock
that the metamorphosis from reality
has been mine.
You are more ancient than I,
and with no avenging lord
to bring pallor to your  cheek
you wear stars in your hair
and the earth murmurs from your eyes.

Forgive me my looming treachery:
for I too will suck on your purity,
joining my breath
with all who breathe on you;
permeating your senses
with the pungency of our morass.
Until then, permit your little hand,
warm and knowing in mine,
to be my transient cosmic link.

# The Trout

Succulent Autumn prize,
dappled quivering flame
lighting the leaf-crisp banks'
ode to winter.
I raise a vicious limb,
the killing stick, poised
ready to describe the quick
destroying arc, twitches with
unease. My eyes held, the
stick stayed by breeding
colours' triumph. Mottled
bronze, clear silver like
trembling spilled mercury
floating perfectly aligned,
red beacons blazing protest
at my dark hunched purpose.
Do I starve? Must procreation
falter at my whim.
One blow, and the sinuous
shaking passion over gravel
is denied him, the milt's
cold blooded cloud will
never settle.

Perhaps years hence (gods willing)
I may repeat this act, be faced
with equal fire, but the mirror
of this murmuring dying
day would shatter with
my swiftly falling arm.
A mouldering leaf invades
the gasping mouth, it is
enough, even the loud stream's
babble chides at me,
the stick is flung aside and
panic grips. As a living symbol
fades with the dripping seconds,
my odd pained hands link to
form the cradle, that swings
existence to the waiting
water's grasp.

# Bryn Celli Ddu

They heaved and levered rock
into the pattern of a mystic dance – a cypher.
A fusion of tomb and temple:
the spiral of stones radiated out,
and swirled in,
to the hieroglyphed slab at the barrow's core,
with the red jasper beneath,
left to smoulder for thirty-five centuries.

And when they felled the great ox,
and buried it there, with its head turned
to watch, always, the maw of the portal,
were they honouring the cosmic mother
and remembering a future
when the primitive magic of science held sway,
observing, perhaps, our benign grave robbers
brush detritus from the scorched bones
of young ancients?

Our conclusion reached (of sacrifice)
reveals only our passion for hideous drama,
clutching at puny parallels
with our shrieking violence,
keeps us uninitiated – even into the first degree,
of exhumed mysteries.

A skull here, a votive object there,
wrapped and despatched . . . trickles of knowledge:
while wisdom lies cocooned
in the moon's and the mayflower's white flame,
and the Goddess gathers dust
in the silence of  countless museums.

## Hill Shepherd, Ton-up Boys

An orhpaned mountain boy content to greet
his twenty-second summer.
He'd worked there from a boy, lived in,
a tousle-headed dreamer.
The creaking farm his teens and manhood haven,
the chimney corner his on yarning evenings
where, drowsy in a soft inebriation,
a  crock of hedgerow nectar swells his fist.
And in the velvet time of owl-claimed hours,
when angry granite outcrops rage at stars,
a bed and cupboard perched amongst the gables
cocoon his somnolent body from the night.

Then in the wild rose sky's pink clouded dawning,
his mind's eye sees again the love-flushed limbs
that twined with his among the secret heather,
the wild silurian girl an aching dream.
Morning hours spent mooning round the farmyard,
gutting tickled trout and robbing hens,
intently watched by opportunist magpies,
bobbing on the gnarled and stunted thorn.

He sets out now, the midday round his purpose,
the customary sack adorns his shoulders:
a hessian-cloaked prince of forty acres
and mountain rights,
drooping pony mounted, drinking the summer wind.
His glass-eyed subjects staring stupidly
watch his passing in trembling awe.
He sees with baleful eye the weekend brigands,
their swift and surly steeds propped at his fence,
mobbing the hide-and-seek winberries,
slogan-painted food gatherers,
back-to-nature townies,
absconders from their teeming  concrete zoo.
"Look at old woollyback over there!"
they point and prance, the Swansea Jacks,
and raise a tipsy roar of  broken laughter

from Baglan fume-fed sandrabbits,
swigging flagons and pissing lead.
He wends his way towards his shimmering hilltop,
hearing the merlin call,
oblivious to the mad despairing taunts
torn from town-soured souls'
subconscious envy.

# Icon

With his visit nearing its end,
he listens to their  carefully spoken words:
irked by the fumble for gentility,
the oblique denial of class,
his discomfort bordering contempt.
Yet, in a vague way, he still fears them.

They sit with him in a room
where nothing  changes.
Below a tapestry
depicting workers in a field
a hungering fire just touches November's chill.

Crystal and brass
gleam in cramped alcoves,
patterned china
softens a dresser's sombre lines.
The piano, tuned, polished,
and mute for twenty years,
stands rigidly obtrusive.

A meal is prepared and served
with the ritual care
of a lifetime's frugality.
Then, at his leaving,
he awaits the final irritation:
his father murmurs
as his mother moves to flick dust
from the dustless icon on the wall:
capped and gowned
his framed youth stares down at them,
the eyes uncertain.

# Transition

No dwellings encrust
the valley's great bowl,
and this church on a bluff
seems almost an intrusion here.
Site of strange rites
with wheaten bread and bland wine,
its arched sockets watch
only the flowered, the feathered,
and the furred.

But Blodeuwedd!
has your whisper persisted:
sharp in the rain's slant,
soft, in the opening buds,
warm as you teased down the sun?
Blodeuwedd! blossom of morning
and feathers of night.

Here on the hill,
in his shell of grey stone,
does Christ hear your song
of flowers?
Could hosts convene for you,
and would he be with them
bright in his manhood among
the flowers of the oak,
broom, and meadowsweet,
the sun in his beard,
there for your coming?

# So Time and Wine

I should get back,
but watch the train depart.
Why do I need this city,
memories perhaps?
For once I'm holding bread
to cast upon the waters,
welcoming an urge to sip luxury.
And there it is,
on the shabby streets' periphery;
a small hotel, select–
and out of place, out of time.

A wine promotion in the bar:
my luck holds, the wine is cheap.
And there we meet,
my accent draws her ear,
and then her stare.
She lowers standards,
engaging me in chat:
"those ghastly miners",
(is every miner Welsh?)

A recent  Catholic convert,
startlingly voluble,
projecting clear pictures
of her frantic social round:
bilingual, of  course–
l'Anglais et le Francais.

"Everything ordained".
By whom, by what? Who or what ordained
the crossing of our paths' instant antipathy?
Ah, you of nurtured life,
you  blame me and my ilk for looming change,
then cut at my desertion of the faith:
could I not see – this gem could be repolished?

I've heard it all  before.

"O ye of little faith".

But why this grasping at the creed I've shed?
What are you buying now,
do you wear this new found succour
like exclusive *haute couture?*
can you hide from life
by shuffling Gods?

Yet, we linger on,
and through grape-mellowing
hours, slowly soften,
seek excuses for the other's madness,
and look each other oddly in the eye.

Will we lay the class war's bedlam
at the dancing feet of lust?
Has time and wine liquefied
the variance in our pride?

"ere the cock crows thrice".
Could I place fifteen shekels on the table . . . ?

Cowed by your nakedness,
reservation stumbles through the door,
leaving us to savour
the peace of touching.
Words a soft encroachment -
you ask for meaning:
let our few brief hours,
leave meaning
to the vine tendrils' grasp.

"And wine was made blood".

Our senses flow
free from love's brutalities,
words stilled,
mouths in ravenous feeding.

O, night made holy
with pleasure's artless purity.

"Mary, mother of God,
pray for us sinners now . . ."

## The Masons

I have seen them leaving.
No chattering throng lingered,
the door opened just enough,
one, sometimes two emerged
then it was closed.
Opened, closed, opened, closed,
like an extended ending of ritual.

But this evening, with the curiosity
of the excluded, I sit, watching for arrivals.
The bench faces the masonic hall;
a muncipal blunder maybe
or some planner's small defiance?

The first to come, I recognise
as a man of the cloth,
now, though, in the half-light,
no white blur marks his throat.
Is this omission
a periodic shedding of grace?
Will Jesus walk arm through arm with him
into this temple, or will the son of God
be left skulking at the door:
omnipotent Mammon, perhaps, irresistible
to the one, somewhat dubious to the other?

# Exodus

I know this valley,
and I too have need
to break bread here again,
share faith with you,
but mistrust lisps at my ear.

Yes! they endure:
their roots are here
and in this
you see hope, strength even.

Yet they wait
for some far-off hand
riffling through papers,
to send a ripple through life here.

Perhaps it is arrogance
frosting my lip
as I mumble blessings
on my own vision
of clamorous exodus?
When even the old
will not pause
at the valley's rim,
or jostle for a backward glance.

Driving home,
there is tension between us,
unleached, like the spoil
sprawled on the hills.

Roadside saplings are shadows
of my thoughts
as they limp from the thicket
into the headlights' beam,
rush forward, then flicker past.

# Allotments

In the repose of suburbia's
easy routines and small intrigues,
he withholds from retrospect,
the people, the party,
his time of ecstasy and despair,
hearing Marx mumbling from the grave
of places at table for the poor.
He rarely looks back,
those passionate years being little more
than an almost anonymous frown
on memory's blurred face.
Propping bean sticks, he looks out
beyond the urban drift
to woods, pastures,
and mountains whose names are evocations:
March Hywel, Mynydd Drymau, Bryn Sidan.
But he does not go there.
A cultivated plot
is his enclosed link with earth
and her moods,
he has coaxed abundance from the soil:
tubers, brassicas, succulents, herbs,
and red currants – scarlet tributes
to his season's work.
Crouching, he feeds a dicarded meal
to the embers of a fire:
beef sizzles,  bread blackens and curls
like the pages of *Das Kapital*,
burned years before.

Elsewhere, sophistry rules
like a resurrected Czar,
and of food, there is much displayed.
Fingers trace the fruit's texture,
nostrils flare to the aroma of fresh meat.
Many indulge this luxury
then buy their rouble's allotment
of bread, some sausage, a few roots.
Here and there,

a defiant red star
moves through the crowd.

On the plot, a hen thrush
fusses amongst the currants,
an airgun is aimed, it is old,
the spring weak:
but power being relative,
snared by branches, beak agape,
the dying thrush struggles.
Blood drips on the leaves below
exploding into small red stars.
He watches, detached now.
Each year there is surplus
and of this, he will not gather,
give or sell.
The currants will rot on the bush;
he has watched them ripen,
cupped their glow in his hand,
he is fulfilled.

Far off, ponderous and confused,
a tethered beast
sways to the rhythm of a new tune.
Millions are entranced by the sound
that holds everything but its own history.
Others bide with the clock's perversity,
hoarding the remnants of a dream,
awaiting the suggestion of a growl
from the great bear's throat.

# The Visitor

Each year she would come,
and for a week
the vale was hers.
She would seek me out
and I, the guide,
could not shake free
as she bored me with slants
on my own history.

What drew her here?

Waterfalls' music was unheard,
as vexed dabbings at the spray
on a face too pretty for comfort
stole the moments.
No flame lit her eyes
as we paused amid colour;
the rockrose, soapwort,
and vetchling,
scarce drew her glance,
she wandered on,
blind to the campions' blush,
and the foxgloves' magnificence.

## Llanberis? Pass

I had the strangest dream
in which Llanberis set the scene
for a politicians' gathering in the snow,
they were Welsh to the core,
steeped in Celtic lore,
(ay, like Vortigern, if you really want to know).
There were many noted climbers
and some hopeful pocket liners
who searched for iron pyrites in the scree,
while the climbers practised falling
(well, it is part of their calling),
but another party really puzzled me.
It appeared they were beholden
to hunt ermine up on Snowdon,
and they squabbled over who should take the lead.
Things got even worse
with insults and a curse
(a rather uncouth way to act, indeed).
Yet, they must have been religious, see,
or that was how it seemed to me
as they poked around the snowdrifts muttering, 'Lord',
while one fell on his knees
in the stiff December breeze,
and prayed for tapping on the shoulders – with some sword.

# Day of the Paddy

Late 1950s, social revolution
     building a dream, houses for all.
Earning a living pushing barrows,
     digging trenches in that haphazard
way of the Welsh navvy.
     Proud of my young strength,
my staying power.
     Spring morning, twelve men
swagger onto the site
     the dipped shoulder, the gimp,
announcing Kilkenny, Connemara,
     and Cork.
Contracted for mains trenches
     needed quickly.
Why use them? We could do it.
     Bastards, taking our work.
Aloof, they ignore our mutterings,
     no need for words:
twelve men, one great arm,
     unfaltering rhythm.
Sweating backs, sinuous muscle
     tearing it out four feet deep,
five hours without pause,
     almost at walking pace.
One o'clock break, great hunks of meat
     fried on shovels
over a spitting fire,
     a loaf per man torn apart.
We watching now, inadequate,
     as we open our small
neat packs of sandwiches.

# Flowering

As colliery manager,
her husband had found Cupid
in the consistency of tonnage.
Enamoured of figures,
he accomplished the movement of coal
with all the finesse
of his pen's excited strokes.
And on Sundays
hugged by his leather chair,
he would peruse the works of Gibbon.

Their garden was her domain.
In springtime, hatted and gloved
and averting her eyes from fornicating nature,
she would tend and replenish.
Bees and flowers were quite safe,
with no obvious carnality in their interaction.

Her odd-job man came twice in each week;
and through the years
she suffered his person,
addressing him only to instruct.
Once, she had found him lopping the hedges,
his lips vivid
through the pit dirt still on him,
and his clothes seeping an odour
of dank places.
Chill with loathing, she had sent him away.
He smothered his resentments,
affecting humility for the payment's sake.
It topped up his collier's wage,
helped fill his glass,
and fund brief interludes
in the arms of some honest wanton.

It is all long past:
they have seen their seasons through,
and here in the nursing home,
bees and blooms are replaced

by the sterility of potted silks.
Yet capricous time,
and their lives' exhausted soil,
have sprouted a final paradox.
Inseparable now,
they shuffle the lengths of corridors,
holding hands, exchanging the kiss of infants,
and sharing incoherence
in the flowering of a strange benevolence.

# Seceders

Devolution?
　Why?
You've shared our flag,
gained a niche
in our short history.
We gave you a squalling,
shield-borne Prince:
arms to wield,
in Ireland, Africa, Asia.
Even allowing you, 'Welisc',
to peer over our shoulders
when we blew sepoys
from the mouths of cannon:
Ah, the roar of the irony.

# The Artist

Part of the local scene,
he'd walk the streets,
filling a bag with
discarded wrappings.
Sat in the pub,
arranging a length
of string to acute angles,
or a pear shape,
sometimes an egg.
He'd watch me intently,
gauging the probability
of a pint,
nodding his thanks -
then ignoring me.
At home one morning,
sounds draw me out
to the garden,
to find him there,
digging a triangular hole.
I bring him coffee, some toast,
then leave him to his trimming.
Later, he's at the window;
I follow him, and see shaped
pieces of red, yellow, and blue foil
laid on the hole's base.
More coffee.
He adjusts, then, with a stick,
a wayward blue shape,
backfills the soil
and marks the angle-points
with three small stones.
It is done – he goes.

That day haunted me,
and in early spring,
I sowed the triangle with
a blending of flower seeds:
then waited through the months,
for the coming of his art.

### Enlistment Drive (1996)

In Cardiff castle
on an Autumn day
a salute is fired
to the glory
of the gallant Welsh,
who are needed now:
Oh, Christ! the same old story.

See boys!

they've closed the mines
and cut our dole,
and now they come – all smarmy –
to tell us again
that we brave lads
are needed in England's army.

Now look here chaps!

we pulled you from
those holes, because we
don't need the coals,
but we'll kit-out each man
and fill his belly:
and if you should doubt
what recruitment's about,
then, watch the last night
of the proms – on English telly.

# Missing

Driving through the hills, you see them,
empty farms surrendered to erosion.
Over the next rise, a gaunt statement
headlines the horizon.
At a slope's end, beyond a thistle-claimed
field alive with finches,
a longhouse sags in briar.

And where are they?
The lone man on the hill's contour,
that woman at the farm door
pitching scraps to a skulking dog,
children in the rain, switching
cattle paused at a ford's turbulence.
No trailers rattle produce to valley towns.

Has the power of the multi-bladed
agro-God reached even into these hills,
to cut away the nuisance
of their poor offerings?

# Breakage

Delicately executed,
wisps of glass drawn from
the shapeless heat,
teased to stalk and head of corn.
A present to a dying mother,
from a daughter stiff with hope.

And Kim, my son,
I watched you weave the miracle of banter
to steal last laughter from your mother's pain,
and saw you step, still masked, into the evening.
Today, relieving me of awkward mundane chores,
your great gnarled hand contacted wrought fragility.

A muted crash, a curse,
a facial earthquake:
though months of fettered tears rise and well,
your mouth is clamped on silence.
Tinklings, from your fingers' quest for salvage,
are a breath of sound misting up my eyes:
I leave you to the gathering of your grief.

# Arrivistes?

What brings them here?
Why leave Middle England's
milksop ease?

Each summer they come,
but first, the hirelings.
Loquacious boyos,  hammer,
hack, and wrench the ghosts
from some abandoned holding.
A radio blares as the yard's
lingering eloquence:
tractor ruts, some hoofprints,
a broken toy,
are smothered by the debris
of two hundred stubborn years.

The hirelings leave
transformation,
and new faces blend
with precursors
who gather, to murmur together:
elegance being foil
to the irritation
of natives chatting loudly
in that alien tongue.

But give them time,
they are not colonists,
where is contrivance,
aggression, strut?
Yet, there is something
that disturbs:
is it the careful insularity,
the nonchalance,
their incurious politeness, perhaps,
or is the aura of quietude portentous:
like the silence in the belly of the Trojan horse?

# The Cry

Relentless disk
above the heat-numbed town;
I know where I must go,
mind and body craving
the quiet and the cool that this place offers.
A hundred yards below the mountain top,
and just above the slapped-down buckling road,
my back is knuckled by the sheep-shorn scrub.
I lay caressed by wind – embracing solitude.

But now an intruder, a man with a stick,
the crazing cambered road tilting him
unwelcome to my mind.
The knee-bent gait, forever climbing hills
even on the flat of market towns.
And his blackthorn extra limb
(that only night can wrest from him,
and prop apart till dawn)
pushes on and up, on and up.
        His world not mine,
and yet I feel an irksome sense of crowding.

A gesture drops the curtain
on these projected thoughts.
No turn of head; his practised
sidelong eyes home in on me,
his stick is held aloft.

'Shw mae'? I call the verbal pittance
of the gawping Anglo Taff.
He steps, swings around to face me,
'Cymraeg, Cymraeg, good Cymraeg I speak;
a lovely afternoon think you.'
The accent: I mark him down as Polish
flotsam of the bloodied tides of war
washed here to lick a living from the granite.
        Subject for a poem!
The gut ache sends me blundering down to meet him.
        He's drunk? a mystery,

34

nearest fiery watering hole nigh on seven miles.
Cymraeg, Saesneg, signs, we weave
the pattern of a conversation.
He speaks of yearly visits to the city;
remarks on changes seen.
'But here' (he nods towards the bleating valley)
'my clock forgot, is rarely set to tick'.

I probe for past, for origins.
He points to a silent struggle,
a continuing stony quarrel;
tenacious grip of farmhouse,
relentless push of mountain.
          'David Lloyd I am!'
Welsh! twenty miles from Swansea,
and I hear this fractured English?
I reap a strange excitement from the fact,
equate him with the stubborn hanging farm,
convey my envy of his brave existence.

The rising of an alcoholic sap
has turned the bulging sinews of his neck
to upland reeds.
Chin touching chest he tries to shake
the anger from his head,
his cap glides away.
'Four years ago I'm giving half a sheep
to lay in drizzle with a village slut!'
Stick stabs at ground, demanding equilibrium,
he lurches, staggers, falls among his stones.
'When do you fuck?' he screams at me.
Sheep raise their heads and leer,
wind stirs triumphant laughter in the bracken
that hugs and hides the sniggering watercourse,
yet flaunts the rich brown flicker
of the loudly ticking wren.
And I am hurtled back through snarling time,
to hear the grunt and scrape of glacial  congress

and feel the shuddering birth pangs of his hills.
Drink-fuelled eyes glow up at me,
his dead fern teeth are nibbling at my mind.
Will he lie with rams regurgitate my thoughts,
gag, and spit them out to gather moss?

He's quiet now, in the trough of vented
anger. Still prone, a song from him in
Welsh; soft and slow.
A palm, hard and brown as rusted metal
smoothes the weathered contours of a stone.
I leave him stroking fur.

# Moon Waxing

I have answered her call.
Though I carry my heart with care,
Unquestioning I came seeking
Her white love.
This field is an island of light.
Peripheral trees hugged by darkness
Listen intently for my heartbeat.
Air sucks at my saliva, and I
Taste her pale breath sweeter
Than colour in this, the moment
Of the soul's primal rapture.
A ring of wounded dreams shudder,
And stars converge as the tongue
Of the mystical voice flicks at
My ear.
Away to the left, a night-hued
Fox rests on his haunches – watching.

# Cathleen

The public bar is full:
crowding faces, supended smoke,
bellowing noise.
Hemmed in my corner
by frantic throngs,
I see you, we smile,
raise hands in recognition.
Cathleen! do you recall a time
when we were young?
My warm advances parried
by tremulous protest:
fear, your unyielding chaperone,
no honeyed words could bribe.
I left you to seek new challenge.
My God, how you changed,
what happened to fear?
You are wearing well,
just a few grey wisps betray
peroxide genie freed,
at grips with time.
Time? Time is short;
short time is what you offer,
'time gentlemen please'.
Your laugh is pitched to gaiety,
there's coyness in your manner,
you gaze through lowered lashes,
the hair flies as you flick your head,
working at allure.
The coquette in you puzzles me.
Why not just lift your skirts
bare your teeth and snarl,
and with aggressive flourish
flash your wares?
Your leering suitors
slobber at the bar
and buy you drinks,
cunt-struck, in an alcoholic haze,
so undeserving of
your brave attempt at mystery.

# Joe

"Some Friday night this, boy," he said,
but did not qualify the statement.
That would come later,
perhaps five minutes; I knew him of old,
this was his way.
He bowed his head and fixed with vacant stare
the patient amber liquid in his glass,
his blue-scarred face like an ancient map,
each coastline a long-past stint
of grunted labour,
exposing the primeval forest
that clawed and snagged
and etched his facial grimace.
In his helmet's light did the oozing blood seem black?
Black as the dancing beams of coaldust
he'd eaten all his life.
I watched him gasp his way toward the bar and back,
spine creaking like a heading prop
as he sat down,
heart and spirit shovelled out ages past,
carted away on the endless drams,
loaded with sunlit dreams, running from his mind.
"Retired, bach, this morning, no more for me.
Let the pinstriped bastards dig it out themselves."
The next Thursday, I followed the hearse,
saw him buried:
in a reclaimed slagheap cemetery.

# The Dancers

Four years and six years:
the sum total of your ages but a decade.
And today you bring to me
the gift of your presence,
lighting this room with your eyes.
"Can we dance for you?"
So offering Tchaikovsky
I await your approval.
Watching, entranced, I marvel as,
unfettered by the guiding hand,
you move with his music.
Movement as fresh as fields,
as old as the earth,
your small arms silk-like in undulation.

The music puzzles you.
"It's Russian" I say.
"Russian? What does Russian mean?"
Ah, little ones, should I tell you
of that vast place of the great tragedies?
Should innocence be blasted
with the reality that may
slowly wind down your dance,
that even now could end with a suddeness
to leave your blithe imprints as recent history?

But your movement continues, soothing me,
causing a prickle of hope on my skin,
and I dream now
of tens of thousands of you
dancing the world's stage,
clear and fluid,
cleansing the festering minds,
hushing the growling throats.

# Dosshouse (1960)

With five pounds' worth of steam used up
and the rattle of the train stilled in my skull,
I make for the town,
wander the darkening streets, find a spike.
Pushing through a basement door,
tired, blasé, and with a poor season's
mud caking my boots,
my pocket chinks the tune of a few coins.
Is there music enough for tonight?

Huge, he sits there, motionless,
a bottle and glass between bare arms
spread across a table.
Light from a popping gas jet,
gives convoluted movement
to the serpents, dragons and naked breasts
inked into his skin.
We talk, haggle:
"You've the look of a Paddy, the tongue
of a Taff," he says – "You long distance?"
He scans my proffered coins . . . nods.

Settling in, sounds pester weariness.
From under my blanket I peer
over supine forms: past the swollen
belly of a cold iron stove
to the room's end where
a row of slumbering old wayfarers,
bandits and madmen
mutter, grumble and groan.

Disquiet fingers me:
how grandiose, modest or artless,
was the substance of each seeker's grail?
Tomorrow, when I leave,
will the shell of my youth linger,
to reserve some dank recess
within this catacomb of a place?

Their quests over, the old ones babble on:
are they now supplicants, or have they found
here, among the corrosion,
a haven for their dreams?

# The Veteran

She helps with his undressing until,
each item at odds,
the creased bundle of clothing is piled
precariously on a chair
as mute testimony to his existence.
Then, burdening his dry bones
with the once-yearly worsted,
she stares with him into the mirror,
seeing only what is there:
the oldest among the old of this place,
trembling through the onslaught of vacancy.
It would be preferable that he stay here today,
quiet, staring at walls.
"But he is one of so few," she is told,
"he is expected . . ."

Once, there had been a time of expectation.
When the masses, girding themselves with realisation,
shook off the curse of acceptance.
But their hour was deflected
by Kitchener's howling eyes,
the finger pointing from every wall,
and the white feather's sickness.

And now, sitting in an always depleted line
with other annual suits, he wishes only for
a dulling of the sun's glare,
not hearing the drone of platitudes and doggerel
as a battle is fought again
through the pinched mouths
of some uniformed bourgeoisie
reliving their fathers' glory.

On his breast glints the row of rewards
that did not ease the blighted years of dissent
following at the heels of the imperialists' war
where he died in his thousands
and saw bright young officers,
fresh from the drawing rooms

of Hampshire and Prussia,
blow each other to pieces
with all the verve of a day at the butts
in the great game
that opened the vein of his revolution,
and kept the drawing rooms,
though sometimes depleted, intact.

# The Village

The road falls gently to a glitter of sea;
breaks in the hedgerows, small stone houses
in twos and threes, veg-gardens at sides and rear
with only the small fronts sacrificed to flowers.
On, from the weathered walls of the old,
the flash and glare of the new.
Spanish-style, pseudo Greek –
they're all here, gardens heaving with colour.
Westmorland, Highbury, The Shires:
anomalous house names slice into the mind:
the crachach invasion is on.

They're building Shangrila
around the old village pub: inside,
not a native in sight, their haunt surrendered
to those who now stare at me . . . coldly.
Appraisal being negative, and intonations easy to mimic,
I order a 'paint of maild'.
Tension evaporates, a blandly smiling cove asks:
'Making for the yacht club, old boy'?
Interest is intense as my voice fills the room:
'Duw, no mun, boy bach, from the valleys see,
I knows nothing of boats'.
The faces freeze, like a crowd of silent skulls.
Inverted snobbery aired, I make for the door,
and that unblemished glitter of sea.

# Returning

To us, this estuary tendered its wide peace,
and the solitude you embraced as
"almost an escape."

I went back to Wales,
to escape everything
but you.

Today, some lingering echo
brings me here,
seeking reflections.

The seathrift is lush just now,
driftwood, warm to the touch,
and larks still burst from the sedge.

But why set all this
as lures
to an image of you?

Is having known you
reason enough
to implicate you in nostalgia?

I have come here, as the sea comes:
covering old ground,
knowing I must go back.

# Notes

Blodeuwedd – "Face of flowers" – from Welsh mythology. A woman created by magic from the flowers of the oak, broom and meadowsweet, who was later transformed into an owl. Research reveals a link with a Goddess-figure more ancient than the depiction of Blodeuwedd, as transcribed in *The Mabinogion*.

Bryn Celli Ddu – bronze age tumulus sited on Ynys Môn (Anglesey). Excavations there revealed the skeleton of an ox, interred just outside the chamber's entrance. Inside, two large pieces of red jasper had been buried at the foot of an inscribed stone. Also found, were the incinerated bones of young people. Originally, the tomb had been the centrepiece of an extensive spiral of standing stones.

Welisc – Germanic word meaning, "Foreigner". Thus, this Anglo-Saxon term for the British Celts became, over time, "Welsh".

# Note on the Author

Born to Irish/Welsh parents in Neath, south Wales, in 1935, Terry Hetherington was a manual labourer for most of his working life: he's been a miner, a steelworker, a navvy, a builder. It wasn't until ill-health and injury forced him into premature retirement in the early 1980s that he developed as a poet.

For two decades Terry Hetherington's has been a distinctive voice not only in the Welsh magazines and anthologies, but in poetry readings throughout the land.